Historical Reenactment

Teaching Tips

Purple Level 8

This book focuses on the phonemes **/er/ie/**.

Before Reading

- Discuss the title. Ask readers what they think the book will be about. Have them support their answer.
- Discuss the book's focused phonemes. Explain that /ie/ has two main sounds: long /i/ and long /e/. Give examples of each.

Read the Book

- Encourage readers to read independently, either aloud or silently to themselves.
- Prompt readers to break down unfamiliar words into units of sound and string the sounds together to form the words. Then, ask them to look for context clues to see if they can figure out what these words mean. Discuss new vocabulary to confirm meaning.
- Urge readers to point out when each focused phonics phoneme appears in the text. What sound does it make?

After Reading

- Ask readers comprehension questions about the book. What is one reason people take part in historical reenactments?
- Encourage readers to think of other words with the /er/ or /ie/ phoneme. On a separate sheet of paper, have them write the /ie/ words into columns by sound.

© 2024 Booklife Publishing
This edition is published by arrangement with Booklife Publishing.

North American adaptations © 2024 Jump!
5357 Penn Avenue South
Minneapolis, MN 55419
www.jumplibrary.com

Decodables by Jump! are published by Jump! Library.
All rights reserved. No part of this book may be reproduced in any form without written permission from the publisher.

Library of Congress Cataloging-in-Publication Data is available at www.loc.gov or upon request from the publisher.

ISBN: 979-8-88996-894-8 (hardcover)
ISBN: 979-8-88996-895-5 (paperback)
ISBN: 979-8-88996-896-2 (ebook)

Photo Credits

Images are courtesy of Shutterstock.com. With thanks to Getty Images, Thinkstock Photo and iStockphoto. Cover – Elnur. 3 – Shutterstock. 4–5 – Boston Globe, Daniel Reiner. 6–7 – meunierd, lindasky76. 8–9 – gnagel, De Visu. 10–11 – gali estrange, OleksSH, Ken Schulze. 12–13 – Sandra Foyt, Gerald Peplow. 14–15 – Katie Dobies, Roman Evgenev. 16 – Shutterstock.

Which of these items have **er** in their name?

When people dress up to recreate events that happened a long time ago, it is called historical reenactment. People take part in reenactments to entertain people and teach them about the past.

For lots of people who do reenactments, it is important to make them seem real. They do not dress in modern outfits or act out things that did not happen.

When they make their costumes, reenactors may refer to real historical outfits in museums. Some people may try to make perfect copies. Some people make them lighter so they can keep them on longer.

If the reenactment is of a fight, reenactors may carry shields and wield fake rubber daggers and spears. These are props that cannot hurt people.

Mock fights are a safe way to see and understand the battles that armies took part in long ago. The reenactors pretend that the people across the field are their enemies.

The armies may yell and shout at each other, but these are not real cries of anger. People understand that it is just acting and that no one is in danger.

If you watch a reenactment fight, you might be concerned if you see bodies on the ground, but do not panic. These are just people who are acting like they have died.

They are following the rules and will get up after the fight. They may have to wait for the people acting as nurses to help them up.

Not all reenactments are of fights. Sometimes, people just spend a few days living as if they were people from the past, such as farmers and bakers.

They may try different activities, such as cooking and farming. They may set up shelters just like the ones people used to stay in.

Historical reenactments are based on real things that happened, but some people go to similar events where they make up their own stories.

For some people, interacting with strangers like this is the perfect way to spend a summer weekend. Even if people do not join in with the role-play, they can still find out a lot about how things were in the past.

Say the name of each object below. Is the "ie" in each a long /e/ sound or a long /i/ sound?

briefcase   pliers

scientist   piece